2 pts ✓

S0-BZQ-667

ARMY RANGERS

BY NICK GORDON

BELLWETHER MEDIA · MINNEAPOLIS, MN

EPIC BOOKS are no ordinary books. They burst with intense action, high-speed heroics, and shadows of the unknown. Are you ready for an Epic adventure?

This edition first published in 2013 by Bellwether Media, Inc.

No part of this publication may be reproduced in whole or in part without written permission of the publisher. For information regarding permission, write to Bellwether Media, Inc., Attention: Permissions Department, 5357 Penn Avenue South, Minneapolis, MN 55419.

Library of Congress Cataloging-in-Publication Data

Gordon, Nick.
 Army Rangers / by Nick Gordon.
  p. cm. – (Epic books: U.S. Military)
Includes bibliographical references and index.
 Summary: "Engaging images accompany information about Army Rangers. The combination of high-interest subject matter and light text is intended for students in grades 2 through 7"–Provided by publisher.
 Audience: Grades K-3.
 ISBN 978-1-60014-824-8 (hbk. : alk. paper)
 1. United States. Army–Commando troops–Juvenile literature. I. Title.
UA34.R36G67 2013
356'.1670973–dc23   2012008558

Printed in the United States of America, North Mankato, MN.

A special thanks to milpictures.com for contributing images.

TABLE OF CONTENTS

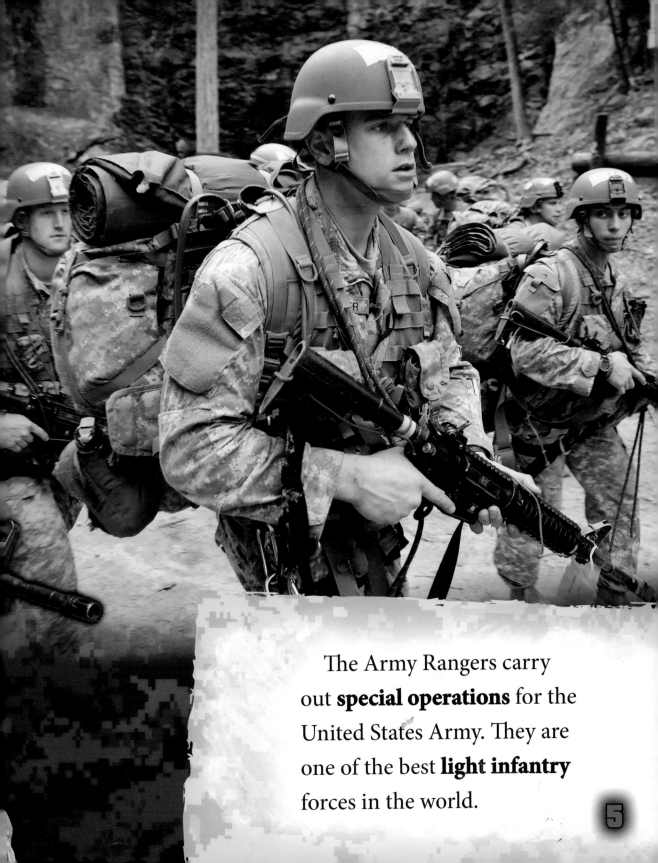

The Army Rangers carry out **special operations** for the United States Army. They are one of the best **light infantry** forces in the world.

75TH RANGER REGIMENT

Founded:	1974
Headquarters:	Fort Benning, Georgia
Motto:	"Rangers Lead The Way"
Size:	About 2,000 active personnel
Major Engagements:	Operation Just Cause, Gulf War, Somalia, Iraq War, Afghanistan War, War on Terror

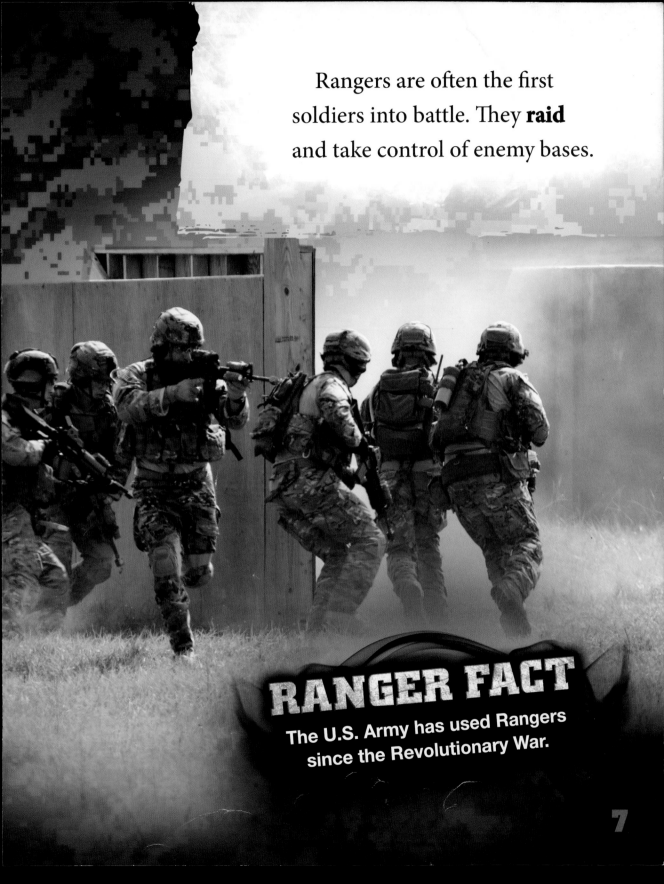

Rangers are often the first soldiers into battle. They **raid** and take control of enemy bases.

RANGER FACT

The U.S. Army has used Rangers since the Revolutionary War.

7

RANGER WEAPONS AND VEHICLES

MACHINE GUN

Rangers fight with many weapons. Machine guns and **grenade launchers** are used against enemy infantry.

GRENADE
LAUNCHER

9

Rangers use anti-tank weapons to blast through thick **armor**. They fire explosives from **mortars** to attack enemies from a distance.

ANTI-TANK
WEAPON

MORTAR

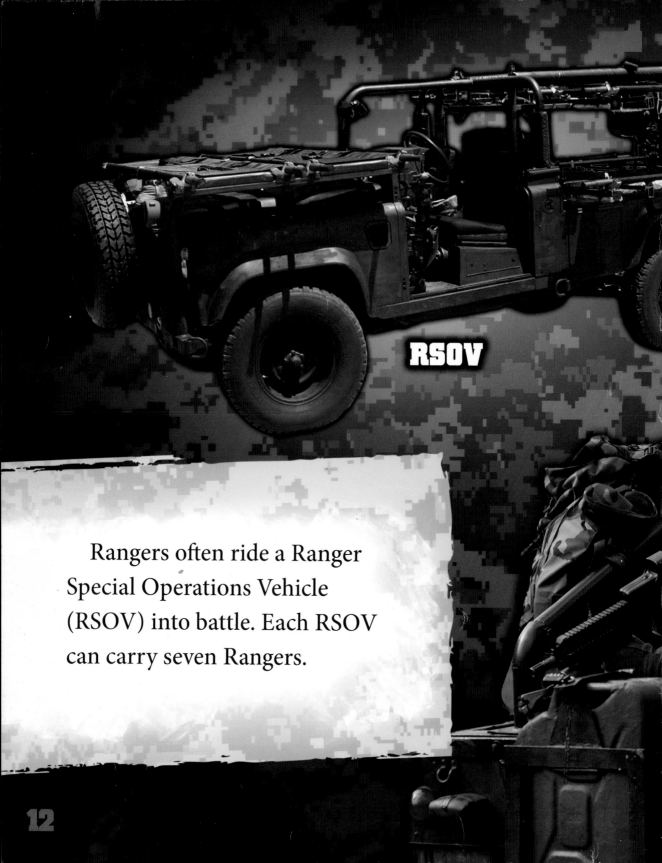

RSOV

Rangers often ride a Ranger Special Operations Vehicle (RSOV) into battle. Each RSOV can carry seven Rangers.

KAWASAKI
KLR250

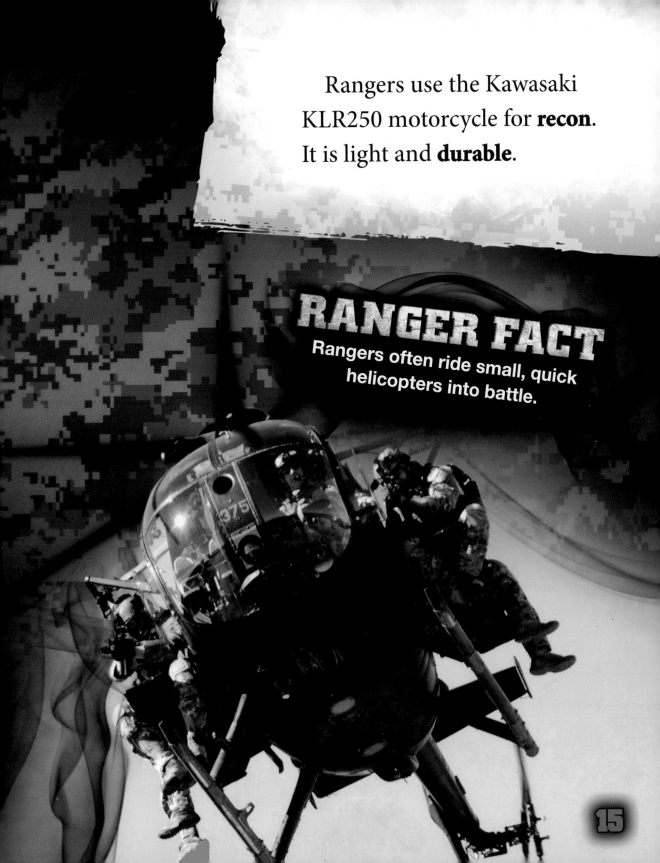

Rangers use the Kawasaki KLR250 motorcycle for **recon**. It is light and **durable**.

RANGER FACT

Rangers often ride small, quick helicopters into battle.

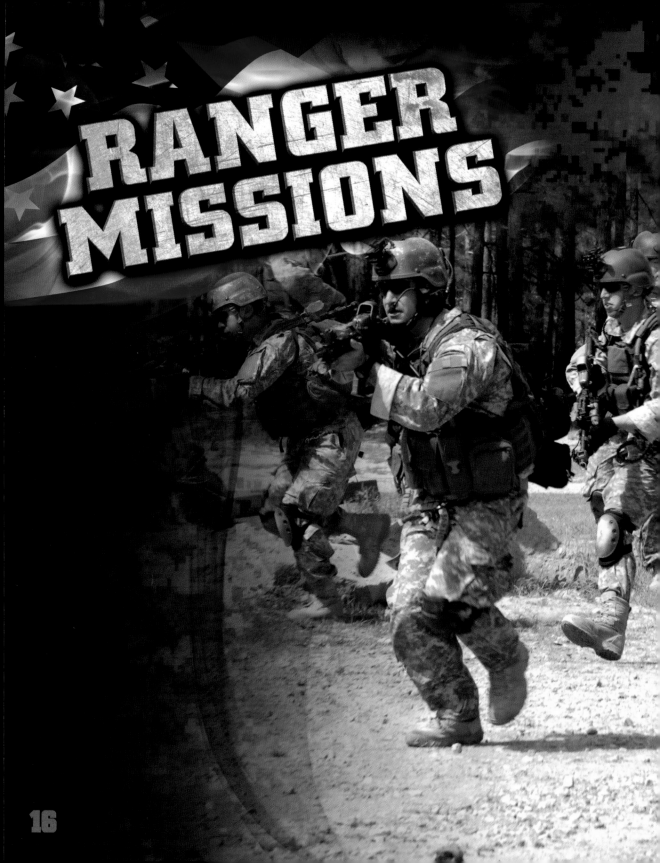

RANGER MISSIONS

The main **mission** for Army Rangers is **direct action**. They perform quick attacks on the enemy.

Rangers often **seize** enemy
airfields. U.S. forces then use
the airfields to launch attacks.

RANGER FACT

Rangers must sometimes rescue soldiers who have been captured by the enemy.

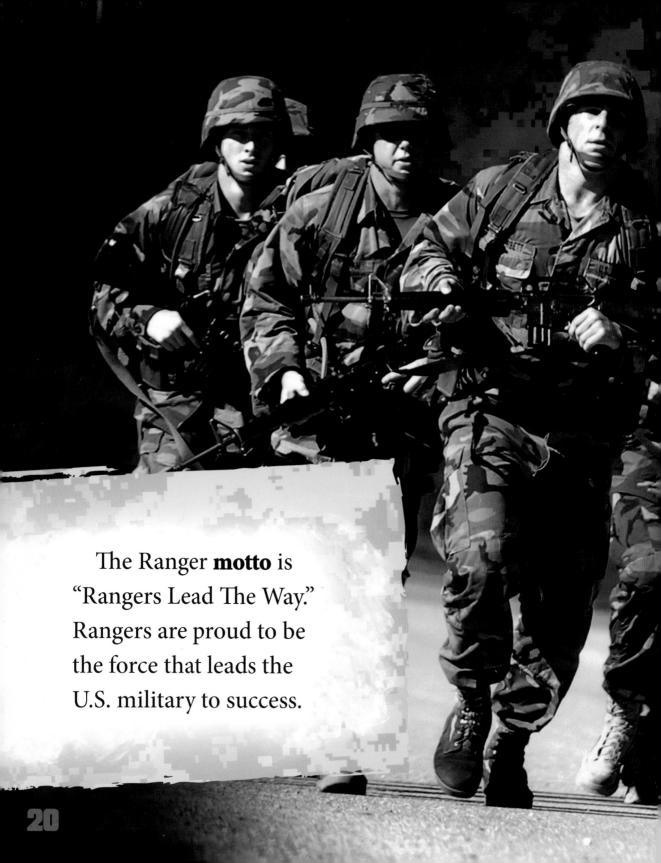

The Ranger **motto** is "Rangers Lead The Way." Rangers are proud to be the force that leads the U.S. military to success.

GLOSSARY

airfields—areas of land where aircraft can take off and land

armor—thick plates that cover a vehicle to protect its crew

direct action—immediate attacks on enemy bases and other targets

durable—tough and long-lasting

grenade launchers—weapons that launch small explosives called grenades

light infantry—highly mobile ground-based troops; light infantry are mobile because they carry few heavy weapons.

mission—a military task

mortars—weapons that launch explosive shells

motto—a short phrase that shows the beliefs and goals of a group

raid—to attack suddenly and quickly

recon—a type of mission that involves gathering information about the enemy

seize—to take control of something by force

special operations—dangerous military missions carried out by a small number of highly skilled personnel

TO LEARN MORE

At the Library

Alvarez, Carlos. *Army Rangers*. Minneapolis, Minn.: Bellwether Media, 2010.

Besel, Jennifer M. *The Army Rangers*. Mankato, Minn.: Capstone Press, 2011.

Gordon, Nick. *U.S. Army*. Minneapolis, Minn.: Bellwether Media, 2013.

On the Web

Learning more about Army Rangers is as easy as 1, 2, 3.

1. Go to www.factsurfer.com.

2. Enter "Army Rangers" into the search box.

3. Click the "Surf" button and you will see a list of related Web sites.

With factsurfer.com, finding more information is just a click away.

INDEX